I Will Always Teach You

Philip Mann

For Madden and Maxi, our two special girls.
Mommy and Daddy love you more than you will ever know!

From the day Mommy told me
you would join us on Earth,
I knew being "Daddy"
would extend past your birth.

I must set the example.
I may even be stern.
I'll do my best to teach you,
and I pray that you learn.

Some lessons will be fun
like learning to talk
or holding your hands
as I teach you to walk...

Or brushing your teeth
as you start to grow,
or tying your shoes
with a knot and a bow.

And as you grow bigger,
I'll teach you to swim,
and shoot that big ball
all the way to the rim.

Riding a bike,
I will show you the way,
and helping with homework,
I'll be there every day.

I'll enjoy all those moments
as you learn to sing songs,
but I also must teach you
your rights from your wrongs.

Some lessons are tougher
and take much more time,
like teaching you patience
and how to be kind.

I'll teach you at playtime
it's important to share,
and when a friend needs you,
how to show them you care.

Respect can be earned
when you treat people right,
and when life becomes tough,
I'll teach you to fight...

Because there are moments,
you will have to be brave.
Giving up in those times
is no way to behave.

But no matter how hard
that life seems to be,
you can always depend
on your Mommy and me.

And if you get angry,
you can let out your ROAR.
But learning to listen,
might teach you much more.

If you listen to God
when you don't know the way,
He can help you through problems
when I teach you to pray.

Faith teaches patience,
wisdom, and love,
and that true happiness
really comes from above.

I will teach you that friendship
is important and great,
but good morals and values
will keep your life straight.

And one very key lesson
will be driving a car,
but you also must learn
just how special you are.

And whether you're good
or whether you're bad,
what I hope you learn most
is you'll always have Dad!

Daddy Loves You.

Me and My Girls

Wife Alexandra and daughters Madden and Maxi.

Dad,

Your role in her life is so much more important than you could ever imagine...

The perfect collection to gift a dad or daughter.

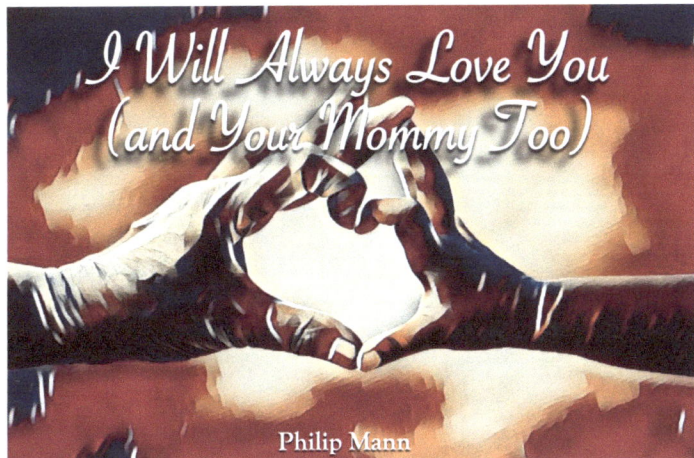

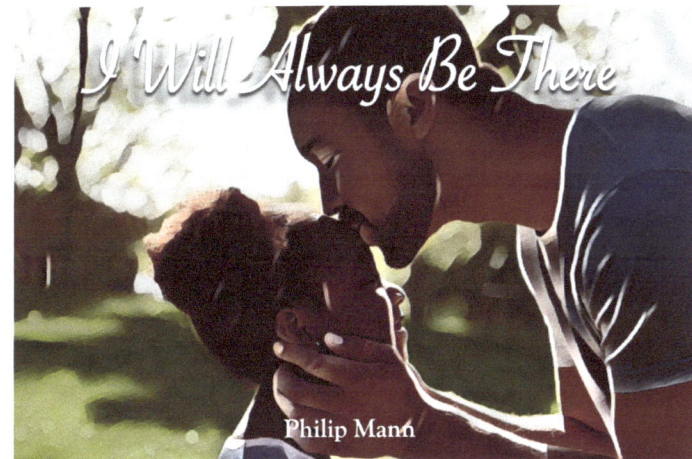

 @philmann10

www.ingramcontent.com/pod-product-compliance
Lightning Source LLC
Chambersburg PA
CBHW042106090426

42811CB00018B/1861